W9-CBD-121

The Story of Nellie Bly

VALUE COMMUNICATIONS, INC.
PUBLISHERS
LA JOLLA, CALIFORNIA

THE VALUE OF FAIRNESS

The Story of Nellie Bly

BY ANN DONEGAN JOHNSON

THE DANBURY PRESS

The Value of Fairness is part of the ValueTales series.

First Edition
Manufactured in the United States of America
For information write to: ValueTales, P.O. Box 1012
La Jolla, CA 92038

Library of Congress Cataloging in Publication Data

Johnson, Ann Donegan.
The value of fairness.

(ValueTales)
SUMMARY: Demonstrates the value of fairness in the life of the turn-of-the-century journalist whose pen name was Nellie Bly.
1. Cochrane, Elizabeth, 1867–1922—Juvenile literature.
2. Journalists—United States—Biography—Juvenile literature. [1. Cochrane, Elizabeth, 1867–1922.
2. Journalists. 3. Fairness] I. Pileggi, Steve.
II. Title.
PN4874.C59J6 070'.92'4 [B] [92] 77-13275

ISBN 0-916392-16-3

Dedicated to Cindy in all fairness

This tale is about a very interesting person, Nellie Bly. The story that follows is based on events in her life. More historical facts about Nellie Bly can be found on page 63.

Once upon a time...
there lived a young woman called Nellie Bly. Nellie was a very good reporter for a newspaper in Pittsburgh—so good that she decided to try to get a job with a really big newspaper in New York City.

But this turned out to be more difficult than she thought. Not one of the newspaper editors in New York would even talk to Nellie, *just* because she was a woman.

"That's so unfair!" she said. "A woman can be as good a reporter as a man." She sat on a bench in the park and tried to think of a way to get in to see the editors. And as she sat there, a thief rushed up, seized her purse, and ran away.

"That really did it." said Nellie sadly. "Now I don't even have any money! I've just *got* to get a job, and right away."

She puzzled and wondered and frowned. But then at last she smiled. "I know!" she said. "I know how I can convince the editor of the *New York World* to give me a job as a reporter with his newspaper."

As Nellie approached the offices of the newspaper, she twirled her lucky ring around her finger. "This time I will make *sure* someone will see me," she said to herself.

What do you think Nellie was going to do?

Nellie walked into the offices of the big newspaper.
"I've come to see Mr. Cockerill," she said boldly.

The guard at the door just laughed. "Mr. Cockerill? The editor? He's very busy."

"Just the same, I want to see him," said Nellie.

"Look here, young lady," said the guard, "I'm here to see that no one gets in without permission. Now go away. Mr. Cockerill won't see anyone today."

"Then I'll wait," said Nellie Bly. "I'll stand right here. Even if it takes all day and all night and all of tomorrow, I'll wait until Mr. Cockerill isn't busy. I intend to see him before I leave!"

The guard didn't like this a bit, but he didn't know what to do about it.

Soon other people noticed Nellie standing there, not willing to budge.

"Who is that woman?" said one man.

"What's she doing here in a business office?" said another. "Why isn't she home where she belongs?"

Nellie said nothing.

She just stood and waited. An hour passed, and Nellie's legs began to hurt. Another hour passed. Nellie began to tremble.

Finally the men began to argue among themselves. They wanted to make Nellie leave, but they didn't know how to go about it. And while they were shouting at one another, Nellie slipped past them and ran into the editor's office.

"What's this?" said Mr. Cockerill when he saw her. "Who are you? What are you doing here?"

"I'm Nellie Bly," she said quickly. "Mr. Cockerill, I want to be a reporter for the *World*. I have experience. I've written stories for the best newspaper in Pittsburgh!"

"A woman reporter?" cried Mr. Cockerill. "Impossible! The *World* doesn't employ women reporters!"

"But that's not fair!" cried Nellie.

Then she stopped and took a deep breath. "Mr. Cockerill, I know that you have plenty of good reporters," she said, "but don't turn me down until you hear what I have to say."

Then she started to tell Mr. Cockerill of a plan she had that was daring and brave. As she talked, the great Joseph Pulitzer, who owned the newspaper, came quietly into the room. He stood and listened to Nellie, and his eyes grew wide with surprise.

"I'll pretend that I'm insane," said Nellie. "Then I'll be sent to the institution on Blackwell's Island where mentally ill people are cared for."

"Blackwell's Island?" cried Joseph Pulitzer. "That's one of the most frightening places in New York. No one knows what goes on there."

"I'll find out what goes on there," promised Nellie, "and I'll write a story about how the poor people at Blackwell's Institution are really treated."

"Very well," said Mr. Pulitzer. "If you can get on that island and write a good report for the *World*, then I'll hire you."

Nellie hurried off to carry out her plan.

First she fooled a group of doctors into thinking that she was insane. This wasn't too hard for Nellie. She was a good actress. The hard part began when Nellie was put into a carriage with a group of women and driven to the institution on Blackwell's Island. She saw the dark, gloomy building, and she began to feel nervous.

"Mr. Pulitzer and Mr. Cockerill know I'm here," she thought. "They said they would get me out. But they didn't say how. And they didn't say when!"

BLACKWELL
INSTITUTION

The doctors and nurses at Blackwell's Island were supposed to help mentally disturbed people get well so that they could go home. "I wonder if they really pay attention," thought Nellie. "I'll try to find out."

So Nellie acted in a perfectly normal way. "I'm not insane," she told the doctor.

"Of course you're insane or you wouldn't be here," said the doctor.

"You're at Blackwell's Island," said the nurse, "and you'll never get out—never!"

The nurse hurried Nellie away to the big room where the patients spent their days. No one there paid any attention to Nellie. She sat down near a battered old piano and tried to feel brave.

"But I'm not brave," she thought. "I'm afraid. It's gloomy here. I wish I had someone to talk with."

At that moment, a little mouse popped out of the piano. "You can talk with me if you like," said the mouse. "My name's Sunny, and I'd like to be friends."

Nellie laughed. She knew that mice can't really talk. She was just pretending that she had a friend in that lonely place. Just the same, she was glad to see Sunny.

At supper time, Sunny scampered along to the table with Nellie. But when the food appeared, both Nellie and the mouse decided they weren't hungry after all.

"Ugh!" said the mouse. "That meat looks awful!"

"And the bread is stale," said Nellie.

Sunny pointed to the nurses' table. "Look at that!" she cried. "They have all sorts of really yummy goodies, while the patients have to eat this terrible food. That certainly isn't fair!"

After supper, the patients went back to the same big, cheerless room.

"Why don't you try playing the piano?" said Sunny. "Maybe the music will cheer these folks up."

"I don't play very well, but I'll do my best," said Nellie. The music did help. Some of the patients smiled. Some of them even sang.

But the smiling and the singing stopped when one of the nurses called out that it was time for baths.

"My goodness," said Nellie. "Why is everyone so upset? There's nothing dreadful about taking a bath."

Nellie soon found that she was wrong. The baths at Blackwell's Island were dreadful indeed. The nurses forced the women into tubs full of ice-cold water.

"Stop that!" shouted Nellie. "You're supposed to be helping these poor people. Instead, you're making them suffer. It's freezing in here. Everyone will catch cold. You're not being fair! In fact, you're not even being human!"

"Aha! A troublemaker!" cried one nurse. "Do you know what we do with troublemakers?"

"I think we're about to find out," said Sunny, "and I don't think I want to watch!"

The nurses threw Nellie into a tub and poured ice water on her head.

"We don't need to be kind or fair," chuckled one nurse.

"No one will ever know what we do," said another.

"You'll never leave here and tell," laughed a third.

"You big bullies!" squeaked the mouse. But no one paid any attention to her.

As the days went by, Nellie began to think that the nurses might be right. She might have to stay forever. "But I'm not sick!" she told the doctor. "Some of these other people aren't sick either."

The doctor just told the nurse to take her away.

"Mr. Pulitzer promised to get me out of here," thought Nellie. "What if he's forgotten all about me?"

Do you think Mr. Pulitzer had forgotten?

He had not.

After Nellie had been on Blackwell's Island for ten days, someone from the *World* newspaper office came for her. "And if you don't mind," said her little friend the mouse, "I'll go with you. I don't care for this place at all."

The doctors and nurses at the institution were very nervous when they found out that Nellie was really a reporter, and they surely had plenty to be nervous about.

When Nellie wrote her story about the dreadful conditions at Blackwell's, people were shocked and angry. "How unfair!" they cried. "What a terrible way to treat sick people. Something must be done!"

And something was done. The city saw to it that the people at Blackwell's Island had warm clothes, good food, and better doctors and nurses who cared about them.

There was a great change at Blackwell's Island, and all because of Nellie Bly.

Nellie's story about Blackwell's Island was the most difficult one she would ever have to write, but it convinced Mr. Pulitzer that she was a fine reporter. He gave her a job at the *New York World*. Nellie went on to write many other stories. And she often used disguises when reporting about people who were treated unfairly.

"You're becoming famous, Nellie Bly," said her little friend Sunny. "Do you know what people are saying about you? Whenever they see unfairness that should be exposed, they say 'Send for Nellie Bly. She can do anything!'"

Sunny was right. Nellie wrote so many stories and she became so famous that other newspaper people became jealous.

"What's the matter with you men?" shouted one red-faced and angry editor to his reporters. "How can you let a mere girl like Nellie Bly get ahead of you every time?"

"Nellie Bly isn't any mere girl," said one reporter.

"In fact, there really isn't any Nellie Bly," said a second newspaperman.

"The *World News* is trying to fool us," declared a third. "They've got a whole team of smart men reporters working on those stories, and they want us to believe they've got just one girl!"

But even Nellie Bly made mistakes. One day she heard that a Broadway producer wanted chorus girls for a musical show. "I'll try out for that job," Nellie decided. "Then I can write a story about how chorus girls are treated. Besides, it could be fun!"

"Are you sure that's such a great idea?" said Sunny the mouse. "Chorus girls have to dance awfully well!"

"It's a fine idea," said Nellie. "Why not? I've had a few dancing lessons."

And Nellie dashed off to get a job in the chorus.

"You'll do," said the stage manager when he saw Nellie. "Here's your costume. Get ready."

"But . . . but what about a rehearsal?" asked Nellie.

"No time," said the stage manager. "Just follow the other girls. You'll be fine!" And he hurried away.

"My word!" said Nellie. "It's much easier to get a job as a chorus girl than as a reporter."

"That's because people think women *should* work in the chorus," said the mouse, "or as housekeepers or factory hands. They don't like it when women want to be reporters. Just the same, this job may not be as easy as you think!"

It wasn't easy.

First of all, Nellie looked sort of silly in her costume, with its helmet and spear and shield. She felt sort of silly, too.

Then, when she followed the other women out onto the stage, she started on the wrong foot. Then she kicked while the others twirled and she twirled while the others kicked. The audience roared with laughter.

"Nellie!" called Sunny. "You're going the wrong way! Stop! Come back!"

"Get that girl off the stage!" shouted the stage manager.

"You'd better stick to newspaper reporting from now on," said Sunny, after it was all over. "I think you have two left feet."

Nellie didn't answer. She was too embarrassed to answer. But she knew Sunny was right.

Nellie never tried to go on the stage again. But soon she had an idea that was even more fantastic.

Jules Verne's book *Around the World in Eighty Days* had just been published. This was the tale of a man who set a speed record by traveling all the way around the world in only eighty days.

In Nellie's day it was difficult to travel. There were no airplanes and no cars. Trains and boats were slow. Most people traveled by horse and buggy.

"No one can *really* travel around the world that quickly," said Sunny.

"Oh, I don't know about that," said Nellie Bly.

Nellie went to see Mr. Pulitzer, and she told him her plan. "I want to go around the world," she said, "and I want to do it in only seventy-five days."

"Impossible!" said Mr. Pulitzer. "It can't be done in that time. Besides, you're a woman, and women simply don't travel alone."

"That's not fair!" protested Nellie. "Men travel alone all the time. Why shouldn't a woman be able to do the same thing? I know I can make it. And think of the exciting stories I'll send back to the paper!"

Mr. Pulitzer thought about it, and at last he nodded. "It would be exciting—perhaps the most exciting story of our time. All right, Nellie, you can go!"

When the other reporters heard about Nellie's trip, they were green with envy. They were also sure that Nellie would never complete the trip in only seventy-five days.

"Mr. Pulitzer should have sent a man," said one reporter. "Women take too many suitcases. That slows them down."

But Nellie took only two dresses and a coat, and she arrived at the pier to catch her ship with only one small suitcase.

"Aren't you afraid?" teased a man. "Traveling this way without anyone to protect you?"

Nellie was a bit afraid, for people had been telling her stories about shipwrecks and pirates and kidnappers. But she wouldn't admit she was scared. She marched bravely aboard the ship with her little imaginary friend, Sunny the mouse.

The voyage was rough, with high seas and gale winds. Many of the passengers were seasick. Nellie and Sunny were very happy to land at Southampton, England.

By this time, people all over the world were reading about Nellie Bly and her fantastic journey. A man from the London office of the *World* met Nellie at the dock. He had a telegram for her.

"Why, it's from Jules Verne!" said Nellie. "He wants me to visit him at his home in France!"

"You can't do it!" warned the man. "You must sail for Italy tomorrow. I have your tickets right here."

"But I can't refuse Mr. Verne!" cried Nellie. "I know it will take time to go and see him, but I'm sure I can make the time up. I'll take a boat to France and then go to Italy by train."

With that, Nellie leaped into a carriage with Sunny, and they dashed away.

Jules Verne was very happy to see Nellie when she arrived at his home in France, but he was a little worried, too. "Should you have come so far out of your way just to see me?" he wondered.

"Oh, yes!" cried Nellie. "After all, if it weren't for your book, I wouldn't be going around the world in less than eighty days."

"That's true," said Sunny, "but if we miss the train to Italy, we may not get around the world at all!"

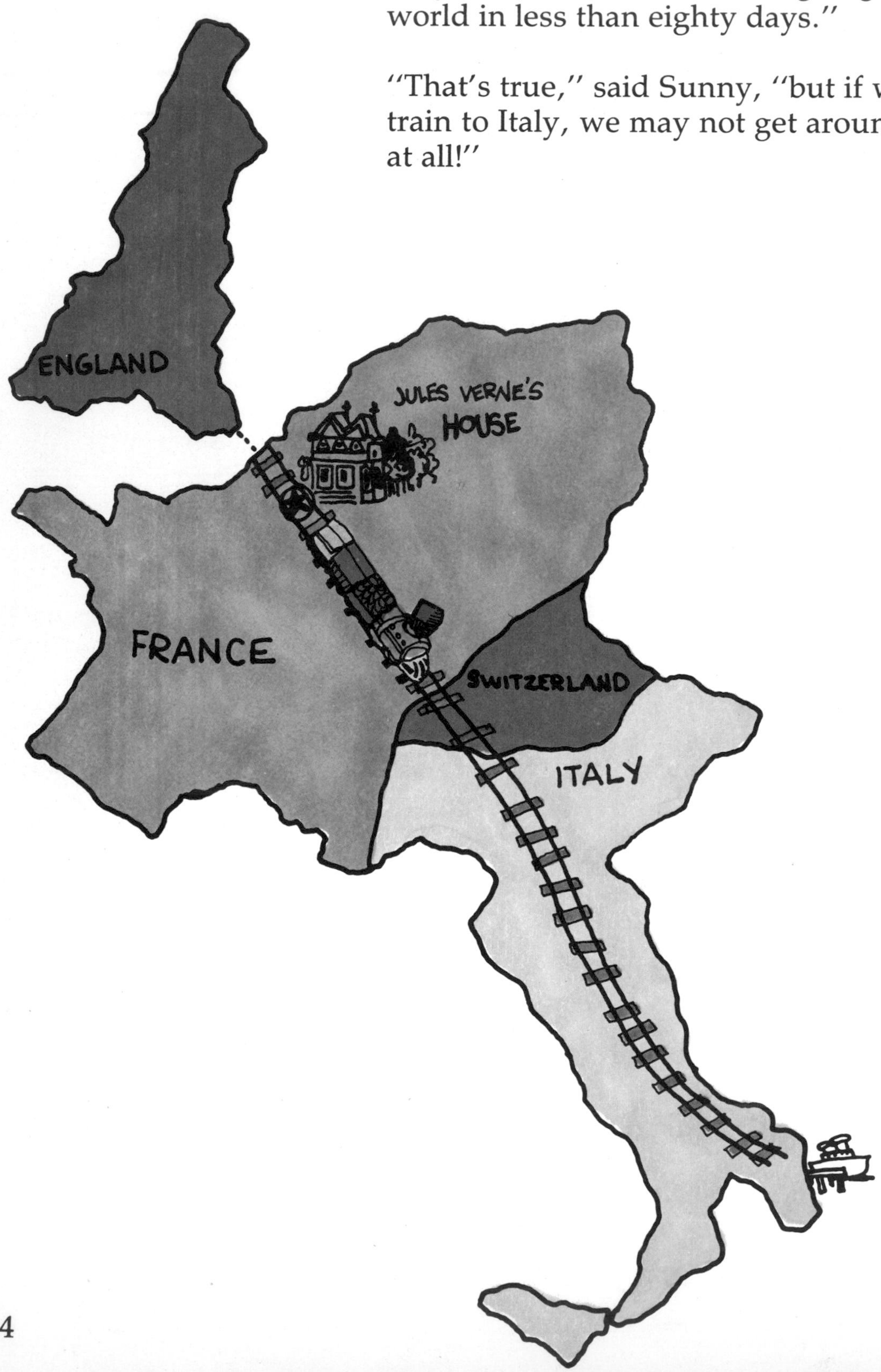

Nellie did not miss the train to Italy. "But what a slow train!" she said to Sunny, when they were halfway there. "We're almost two hours behind time. We're sure to miss the ship for Japan!"

"Oh, no!" cried Sunny. "How will you ever face Mr. Pulitzer?"

Nellie was really upset when the mouse said that. She knew that Mr. Pulitzer was depending on her, and that all the newspapers were following her trip day by day. "Perhaps I shouldn't have been so stubborn about going to see Mr. Verne," she said.

When the train reached her destination in Italy, Nellie hired a carriage to take her to the wharf. "But it's really no use going on," she said to the mouse. "See how late it is! I'm sure the ship has already sailed."

Sad and disappointed, Nellie sank back against the cushions of the carriage and buried her face in her hands.

But suddenly, Sunny cried out, "Nellie, look!"

Nellie sat up and opened her eyes. She couldn't believe it. The ship she had to take was still at the pier.

"Whoopee!" shouted Nellie. She leaped out of the carriage. She tossed a whole handful of money to the driver. Then she ran as fast as she could up the gangplank to the ship.

There was no way Nellie could have known, but her train from France had carried important mail. The mail had to be loaded onto the ship, and so the ship had waited for the train.

The ship left Italy and sailed eastward toward the Suez Canal and the Red Sea. All along the way, Nellie wrote stories about her trip—about the strange new lands she saw where people talked and dressed so differently from the people back home.

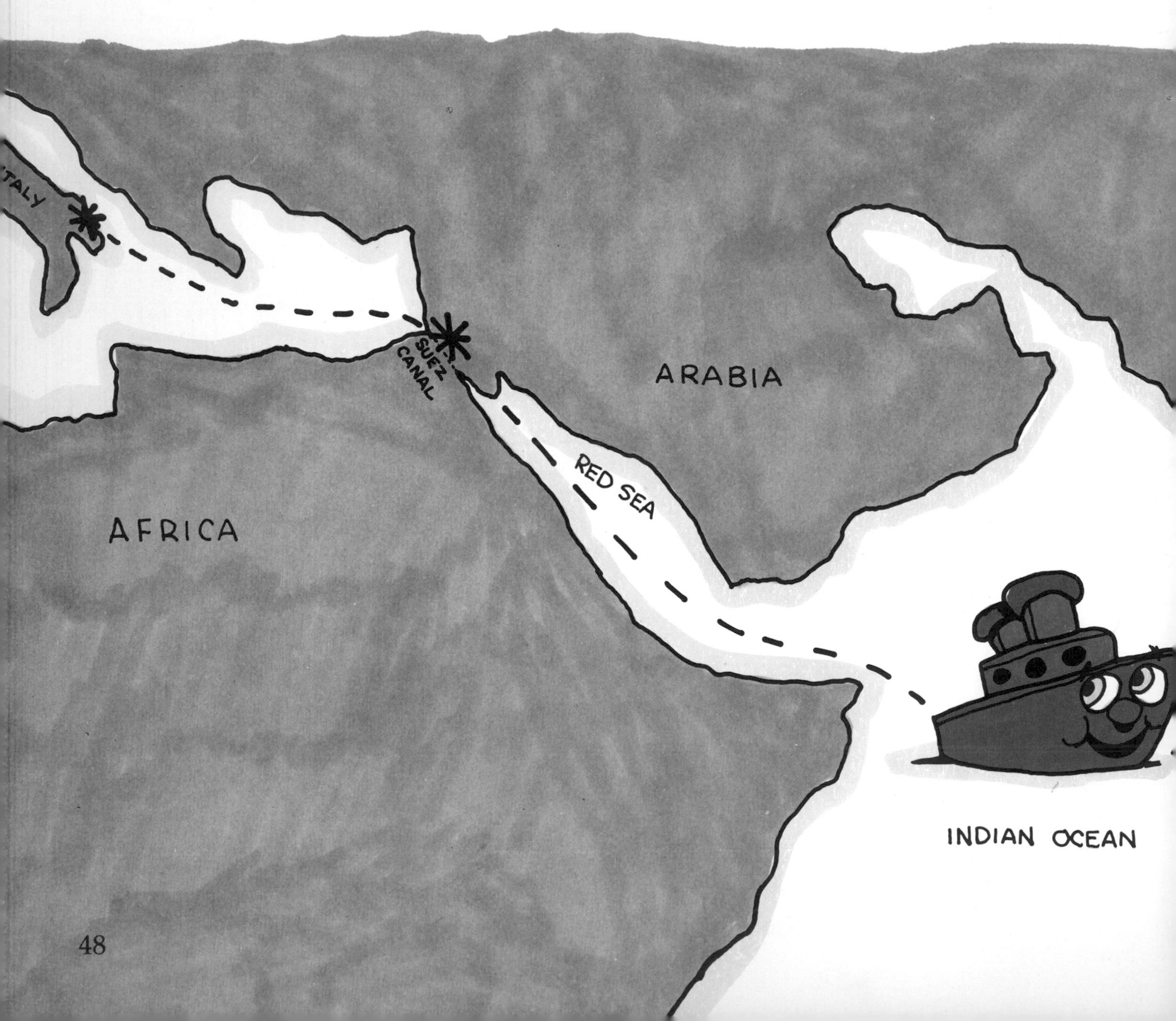

Nellie was very happy. Her ship left the Red Sea and sailed into the Indian Ocean, headed for the island nation of Ceylon. But then a terrible storm slowed the ship down. And when Nellie reached Ceylon, she was behind schedule.

"You have to make up time again," warned the mouse.

"I know. We'll do it somehow," said Nellie. And they sailed from Ceylon to Singapore.

When she reached Singapore, Nellie had gone halfway around the world. She stopped and bought a monkey. ''Even if I'm late reaching home,'' she said, ''this monkey is proof that I've been in this strange land.''

Sunny the mouse laughed. ''After this, people won't be able to say women can't do things,'' she predicted. ''They won't be so unfair.''

From Singapore, Nellie traveled on to Yokohama, Japan. There, hundreds of people came to watch her and her monkey board the ship that would take her back to the United States.

"They're cheering for you," said the mouse. "They're hoping that you'll set a speed record."

"I hope so, too, but we're behind schedule," said Nellie.

On the third day of Nellie's voyage home, trouble began. Huge storms tossed the ship about. Waves crashed onto the decks, and high winds blew the ship off its course. The passengers were terribly frightened, and even the sailors were scared.

"Your monkey is a jinx!" said the crewmembers to Nellie. "Everyone knows it's bad luck to have a monkey on a ship. You'll have to throw it overboard. Then the storm will stop."

"That's not fair!" said Nellie. "It's silly, too. How could a monkey cause a storm?"

What do you think happened to the poor monkey?

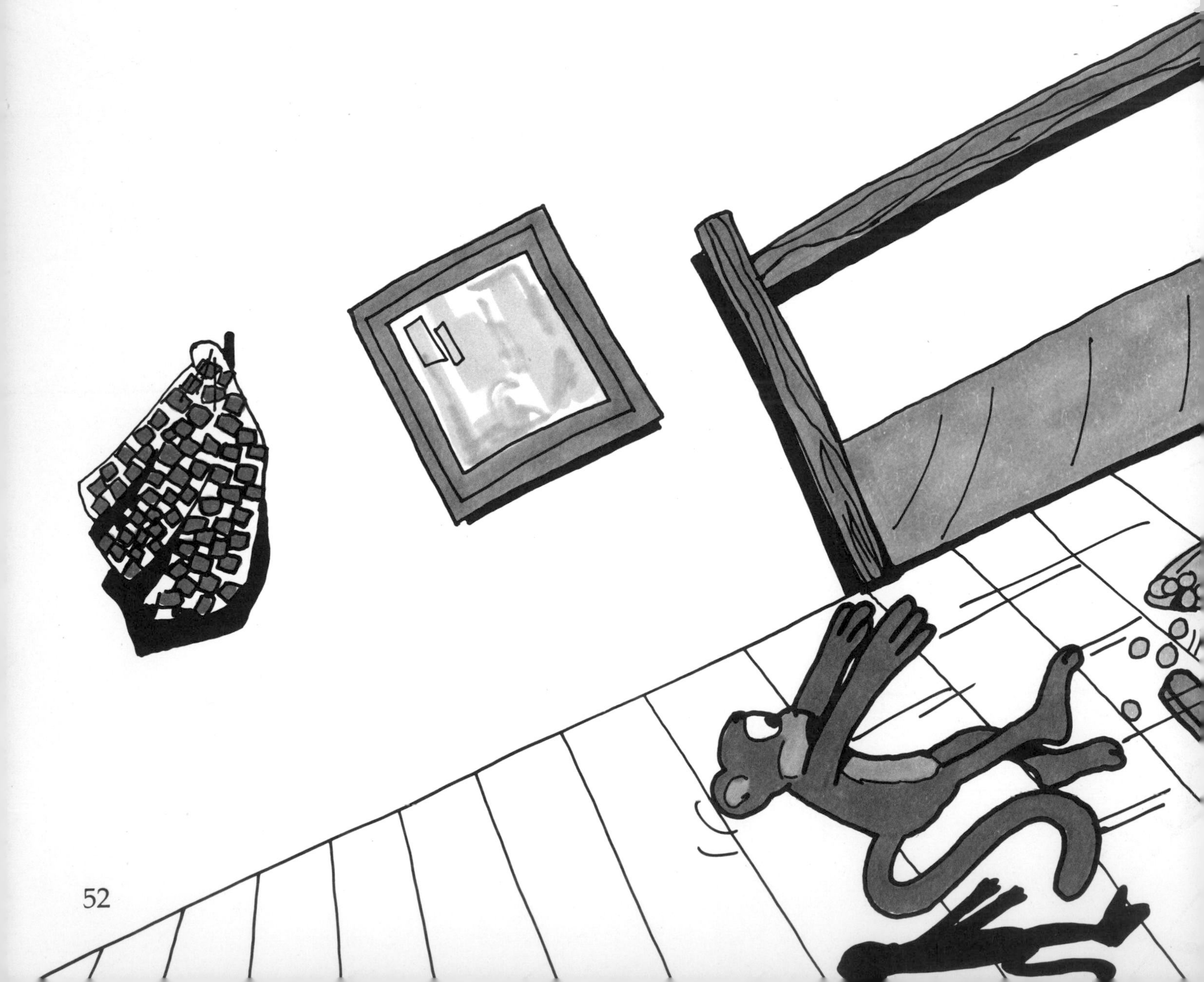

Nellie went straight to the captain.

"I will not throw my monkey overboard," she said. "It isn't fair to expect me to do that. The monkey has nothing to do with the storm."

Luckily, the captain wasn't superstitious. "Of course it isn't fair to ask you to throw your monkey overboard," he said. "Keep the monkey, but keep it hidden so the crew won't be frightened."

After two weeks of difficult sailing, Nellie's ship came into sight of land. "There's San Francisco Bay at last!" cried Nellie.

"And I see that the crowds have been waiting for you," said the captain. "But I'm afraid I can't let you land. There's a rumor that there's a case of smallpox on board, and the health officials want to make certain everyone's well before they leave the ship."

"But I must get off!" cried Nellie. "I have no time to waste. I'll jump overboard and swim if I have to!"

Do you suppose Nellie really did jump overboard?

Well, the captain believed she would. So he found another way for her to land. In no time, Nellie and her monkey, and of course her little friend the mouse, were aboard a tugboat, puffing toward the San Francisco waterfront.

"There's a doctor waiting at the pier to examine us," said Nellie. "We won't lose any more time now!"

Hundreds of people crowded the dock to cheer for Nellie as she stepped ashore. Bands played and people sang. "For sixty-eight days I've been hurrying around the world and now I'm back in America again," said Nellie happily. "There's no place like home!" Then she climbed into a carriage to be whisked off to the railroad station.

But Nellie's race against time wasn't quite over. She still had to cross the continent and get to the East Coast, where the journey had begun.

Cowboys and Indians, ranchers and farmers, came from miles around to see her special train speed by. At every stop, people crowded around the train to cheer Nellie on and to stare at the monkey she had brought all the way from Singapore.

And when she arrived back home again, there were thousands and thousands of people waiting for her. "She's won! She's done it!" they shouted. "Nellie Bly has gone around the world in seventy-two days!"

Nellie's little friend the mouse laughed gleefully. "They never thought you'd do it," she said. "They thought you'd give up, just because you're a woman."

Nellie was terribly excited by the cheers and the crowds. But there was one person she was especially eager to see.

Do you know who that was?

It was Mr. Pulitzer, of course.

"I'm proud of you," said Mr. Pulitzer. "Not only have you won your race against time, but you've shown people everywhere that a woman can take care of herself wherever she may go."

"Welcome home, Nellie Bly!"

Nellie was very happy, and not only because she had won her race against time. She was happy because she knew that many people would now be treated more fairly because of what she had accomplished as a newspaper reporter.

Think about it. Then ask yourself how fair you are in the way you treat others. Do you believe that fairness is important? Do you think it could make your life happier, too?

Historical Facts •

Nellie Bly was born Elizabeth Cochrane in a small town in Pennsylvania. She was a frail girl and her large, muscular brothers teased and tormented her. She learned at a young age to be daring; anything they could do, she tried to do better.

When Elizabeth's father died, she and her mother moved to Pittsburgh. In 1885, not yet twenty years old, Elizabeth, who wanted to become a writer, read an article in the *Pittsburgh Dispatch* titled, "What Girls Are Good For." At this time, women were not allowed to vote, and only a few jobs were available to them. The article was strongly opposed to women's rights to vote and to have careers outside the home. Elizabeth was infuriated and wrote a stinging rebuke to the editor.

George Madden, who had written the article, was so impressed by the anonymous letter that he ran an advertisement asking the writer to contact him. Madden wanted to hire the writer as a reporter for his newspaper, but when he discovered that Elizabeth was a woman, he almost changed his mind. In spite of himself, though, he offered her a job. Elizabeth's name, however, could not appear on the articles she would write. She had to use a pen name, so she chose Nellie Bly, taken from a popular song by Stephen Foster.

Nellie wanted to write from first-hand experience about social inequity. She went into Pittsburgh's slums, factories, hospitals, orphanages, and prisons. And she wrote about all the dismal working and living conditions she encountered. Her exposés engaged public interest but enraged the businessmen who ran the places she wrote about. Madden encouraged Nellie to take a vacation.

Nellie headed for New York, where she was turned away from many newspapers solely because she was a woman. Finally, she convinced Joseph Pulitzer and John T. Cockerill to put her on the staff of the *World*. She promised them a story about the city's insane asylum, Blackwell's Island.

Nellie's sensational Blackwell's Island story prompted an investigation. Reforms were initiated and the city improved the institution.

But Nellie was just beginning. Disguised, she exposed fraudulent employment agencies. She framed herself on a theft charge with a friend and got arrested. She wrote about the injustices to women prisoners. She threw herself off a ferry boat to test the efficiency of the rescue crew. She exposed a corrupt lobbyist. And she encouraged women to demand their rights.

NELLIE BLY
1867–1922

Still no one knew Nellie's true identity, and many people believed Nellie Bly was really a team of men reporters.

Around the World in Eighty Days by Jules Verne was a popular book in the 1880s. Nellie wanted to outdo the speed record set by Verne's fictional hero Phileas Fogg. Pulitzer thought it was a good idea but wanted to send a man. When Nellie said she would take the trip for another newspaper, Pulitzer relented.

She set out from New Jersey on November 14, 1889, and arrived back in New Jersey exactly 72 days, 6 hours, and 10 minutes later. She had beaten the record.

Nellie continued to write articles for the *World* until 1895 when she married Robert L. Seaman, a New York businessman. They lived quietly in New York until Seaman's death in 1910.

Nellie was in Austria during the outbreak of World War I. She returned to the United States in 1919, and was hired by the *New York Journal*.

When Nellie died three years later of pneumonia, the *Journal* paid her a tribute she would have been proud of. It said ". . . she was considered the best reporter in America."

Other Titles in the ValueTale Series

THE VALUE OF BELIEVING IN YOURSELF	The Story of Louis Pasteur
THE VALUE OF DETERMINATION	The Story of Helen Keller
THE VALUE OF PATIENCE	The Story of the Wright Brothers
THE VALUE OF KINDNESS	The Story of Elizabeth Fry
THE VALUE OF HUMOR	The Story of Will Rogers
THE VALUE OF TRUTH AND TRUST	The Story of Cochise
THE VALUE OF CARING	The Story of Eleanor Roosevelt
THE VALUE OF COURAGE	The Story of Jackie Robinson
THE VALUE OF CURIOSITY	The Story of Christopher Columbus
THE VALUE OF RESPECT	The Story of Abraham Lincoln
THE VALUE OF IMAGINATION	The Story of Charles Dickens
THE VALUE OF SAVING	The Story of Benjamin Franklin
THE VALUE OF LEARNING	The Story of Marie Curie
THE VALUE OF SHARING	The Story of the Mayo Brothers
THE VALUE OF RESPONSIBILITY	The Story of Ralph Bunche
THE VALUE OF HONESTY	The Story of Confucius
THE VALUE OF GIVING	The Story of Ludwig van Beethoven
THE VALUE OF UNDERSTANDING	The Story of Margaret Mead
THE VALUE OF LOVE	The Story of Johnny Appleseed
THE VALUE OF FANTASY	The Story of Hans Christian Andersen
THE VALUE OF FORESIGHT	The Story of Thomas Jefferson
THE VALUE OF HELPING	The Story of Harriet Tubman
THE VALUE OF DEDICATION	The Story of Albert Schweitzer
THE VALUE OF FRIENDSHIP	The Story of Jane Addams
THE VALUE OF ADVENTURE	The Story of Sacagawea